CHIRP

The UNHURRY Book

Lara Bryan, Alice James and Eddie Reynolds

Illustrated by:
Freya Harrison

With expert advice from:
Dr Angharad Rudkin,
Clinical Child Psychologist at the
University of Southampton

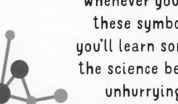
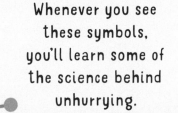

Whenever you see
these symbols,
you'll learn some of
the science behind
unhurrying.

TAKE TIME TO UNHURRY

A lot can happen in a day. However much you pack in, psychologists think that taking some time out every day to have a quiet moment can help keep your brain happy and healthy.

Whether it's five minutes, half an hour or an afternoon, this book is about taking TIME to do something peaceful, to put busy thoughts to one side, and to enjoy the moment.

The activities in this book are known as RELAXATION TECHNIQUES. Give them a go, and see which ones work best for you.

They have all been recommended by a psychologist – someone who studies people's brains and behaviour.

2

INSIDE THIS BOOK YOU'LL FIND...

...ALL SORTS TO WRITE, COLOUR AND DRAW

Lose yourself in a story
(see pages 38-41)

Shade in soothing squiggles
(see pages 20-21)

Paint gently rippling waves
(see pages 44-45)

Stand tall like a tree
(see pages 18-19)

...WAYS TO MOVE AND BREATHE

Breathe in, and out, and in... and out...
(see pages 26-27)

Make a cosy den
(see pages 48-49)

Fold an origami dove
(see pages 56-59)

Try some quiet meditation
(see pages 32-33)

...STUFF TO MAKE AND DO

I am a sloth. We're slow, slow creatures that can teach you a thing or two about unhurrying...

Watch an "unhurry" jar swirl
(see pages 8-9)

USBORNE QUICKLINKS

For links to websites where you can find more relaxing things to do, from calm breathing and crafts to watching videos of slow-moving sloths, go to usborne.com/Quicklinks and type in the keyword UNHURRY. Please follow the online safety guidelines at Usborne Quicklinks. Children should be supervised online.

PEACEFUL PALETTE

The colours on this page are traditionally associated with feeling calm and relaxed.

Try coming up with a peaceful name for each colour - something that reflects what it looks like, or how it makes you feel.

LAVENDER BREEZE

SOFT PINK

SLEEPY PURPLE

WARM GLOW

ELEPHANT'S EARS

There's some space here for you to add your own colours. Do you have any pencils, chalks or paints you think look peaceful?

Unwind by decorating this pattern with some peaceful colours.
You could use the ones on the left-hand page for inspiration.

HERE AND NOW

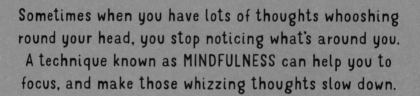

Sometimes when you have lots of thoughts whooshing round your head, you stop noticing what's around you. A technique known as MINDFULNESS can help you to focus, and make those whizzing thoughts slow down.

Being mindful is all about noticing what's happening NOW. Wherever you are, note down a few things you can SEE, SMELL, FEEL and HEAR.

I can
SEE...

I can
SMELL...

I can
FEEL...

I can
HEAR...

Try it around your house. Wander from room to room,
and jot down things you see, smell, feel and hear.

I can SEE...	I can SMELL...	I can FEEL...	I can HEAR...

Some scientific research suggests that practising mindfulness regularly can change your brain. It can decrease the size of the part of your brain that makes you feel stressed. This part is known as the AMYGDALA. It can also thicken the part of your brain that increases your concentration and awareness – your PRE-FRONTAL CORTEX.

UNHURRY JAR

Make yourself an "unhurry" jar, and watch glitter swirl and sink every time you need to settle your thoughts. Look out for BIODEGRADABLE glitter. That way, if you come to throw it away later, it won't harm the environment.

1 Clean out a clear, empty jar. Make sure it's got a lid.

You can use any jar – glass or plastic – as long as the sides are see-through.

2 Fill it with water, and a few drops of food dye...

3 ...then add lots of GLITTER.

Biodegradable glitter is made from plants. It will say if it's biodegradable on the packet.

4 Screw on the top tightly.

You could add sticky tape around the lid too so it doesn't leak.

SHAKE or SWIRL the jar.

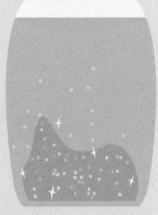

Think of the glitter in the jar as your busy bustly thoughts. Watch the glitter settle down, and imagine all those thoughts doing the same.

If you don't have a jar, you could add some of your thoughts here.

Put them on these pink patches, and imagine them settling down.

You could write words, sentences, or even draw out what you're thinking.

Colouring can help you relax, by giving you something to focus on.
But different ways of colouring suit different people, in different moods.
Which of these two techniques do you prefer?

SLOW AND STEADY

Fill in this pattern with any colours you like, but do it as slowly and carefully as you can.

FAST AND LOOSE

There's only one aim here: Fill this WHOLE page with COLOUR. HOW and WHAT you draw is up to you.

Swirls

Scribbles

Dots

You might find that slow, precise colouring feels more relaxing one day, and free scribbling feels better the next. All that matters is that it helps you relax and slow down.

A PLACE FOR CALM

Draw and design a peaceful place – a room specially designed to help you RELAX and UNWIND. Whenever you feel flustered, visit the room in your mind and imagine relaxing inside it.

The more you imagine the room, the more it will help. Scientists call this CONDITIONING. You'll train your body to calm down whenever you imagine you're here.

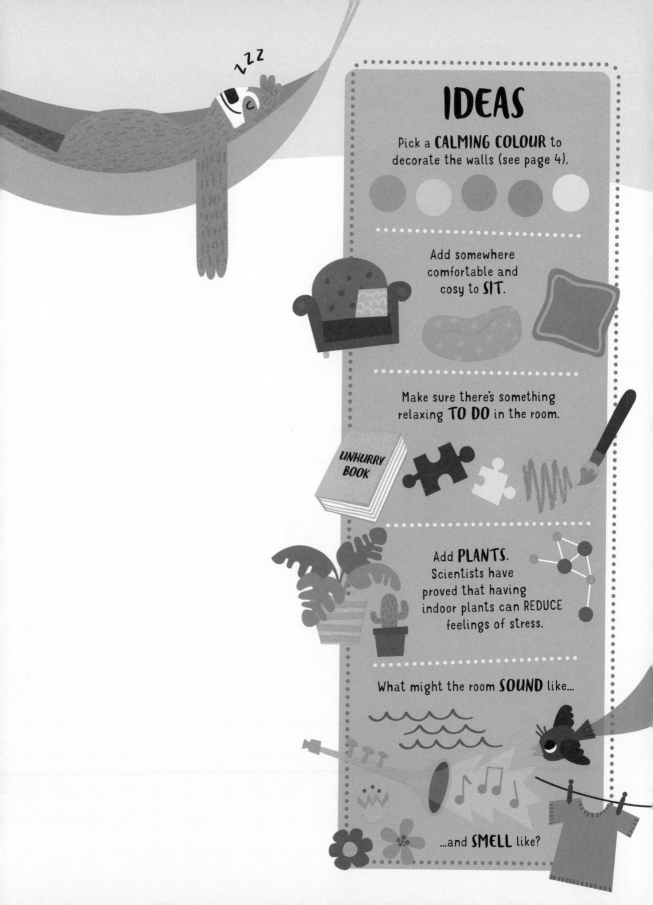

IDEAS

Pick a **CALMING COLOUR** to decorate the walls (see page 4).

Add somewhere comfortable and cosy to **SIT**.

Make sure there's something relaxing **TO DO** in the room.

UNHURRY BOOK

Add **PLANTS**. Scientists have proved that having indoor plants can REDUCE feelings of stress.

What might the room **SOUND** like...

...and **SMELL** like?

HAIKUS

HAIKUS are ancient Japanese poems, made
up of 3 lines of 5, 7 and then 5 syllables.
They are relaxed poems, with no rhyme.
Haikus are usually about seasons,
or the time of year.

5 SYLLABLES
in the first line

3 LINES

Snow falls, people wait
lights twinkle in warm windows
as cold blows outside.

7 SYLLABLES
in the second
line

5 SYLLABLES
in the third line

Trees are flowering
buds burst along tree branches
pink, magenta, white.

Take some time to compose
your own haikus here. You could
think up different haikus for
different times of year.

TRAFFIC LIGHTS

BEEP BEEP

If it feels very busy inside your head, with thoughts whizzing and rushing around, you could try using this traffic lights system to work out how you feel, and how to feel better. You can use it by yourself, or you might find it easier to share with someone else.

If your head is full of difficult, busy thoughts, and you're finding it hard to be calm, you can say you feel **RED**.

Feeling red means it's time to STOP. Take some time to breathe, relax and switch off.

If you're feeling a little worried, or on edge, you can say you feel **YELLOW**.

If you feel red or yellow, take time to do some of the activities in this book – or anything else that helps you slow down.

If you're feeling lovely and calm, you can say you feel **GREEN**.

Most people feel red and yellow sometimes, and that's OK. If you find you feel red almost all the time, talk to a grown-up you trust.

Saying RED, YELLOW or GREEN can be a lot easier than trying to explain how you feel. It can also help the people around you understand how you're feeling, and perhaps how they can help you.

Have a go at using the traffic lights here.

What colour are you feeling right now? Colour it onto one of these traffic lights.	If you're red or yellow, take some time doing an activity. Which one did you try?	How did you feel afterwards? Mark it in here.

You might find different activities useful, at different times. Remember relaxation techniques can take a little practice – just like riding a bike or playing a guitar. The more you do them, the better at them you'll become.

17

BE LIKE A TREE

When trees bend and sway in the wind, their roots keep them balanced and strong. Try this tree sequence used in YOGA – an ancient practice that focuses on strength, flexibility and breath.

1 MOUNTAIN

Start standing up straight and tall.

Let your shoulders relax.

It's best to do yoga barefoot, with lots of space around you.

Keep your head still and your body straight and strong – like a mountain – to help you balance.

2 SWAYING PALM TREE

Link your fingers together, stretch your arms up and bend your body to one side, then the other.

Psychologists think feeling rooted and connected – whether to the place you live, the people you're around or even the ground beneath your feet, can help you feel calm and peaceful.

Feel your feet rooting you to the ground as you sway.

3 TREE

Go back to mountain pose and lift one foot onto the other.

Breathe in and out steadily through your nose to help you feel super relaxed while you're doing yoga.

Bring your hands together in front of your chest.

Then try lifting your top foot higher on your leg until it's just below or above your knee. Rest it there...

...then lift your arms above your head as if they were branches.

See how long you can balance. Then try the tree pose on the other side.

To help you balance, pick a spot in front of you to focus your eyes on. Don't worry if you wobble, that's part of the pose.

SOOTHING SQUIGGLES

Take some time out to colour in this squiggle.
Try to make sure no touching shapes are the same colour...

Mathematicians say you only need FOUR colours to fill in any pattern like this, without a colour touching the same one at any point. Can you make this work?

Colour slowly,
and deliberately.

Create your own big squiggle here. Then slowly, carefully, fill it in. The smaller the shapes are, the more intricate and elaborate the pattern will be.

SENSE SAFARI

If your head is full of noise, try a distracting SENSE SAFARI. When you are outside, focus on what you can SEE, SMELL, HEAR and FEEL. You could write it down on this page.

Notice COLOURS, PATTERNS and SHAPES.

Open your eyes wide. What can you **SEE**?

Look at people ambling...

...animals sunning themselves...

...or plants blowing in the wind.

What can you **SMELL**?

Cut grass

This is an example of MINDFULNESS. There is more information about it on page 6.

Flowers

Blossom

22

GRRR

Traffic rumbling

HMM

CHIRP
TWEET
CHEEP

Birds
tweeting

Water
dripping

PLINK

DROP

What can
you **FEEL**?

Hot sun

Leaves
crunching

Now try
listening.
What can
you **HEAR**?

Chilly wind

The clothes
you're
wearing

A breeze

Taking a MINDFUL walk
can help RECHARGE your
brain, freeing it up and
making it easier to focus.

Rain

23

BUGS AND BEETLES

Decorate all these creepy crawlies. Do them one by one, and take your time.

Find another beetle identical to this one.

BREATHE IN...
...AND OUT

In stressful situations, taking deep breaths IN through your nose and OUT through your mouth, can help you keep calm.

SLOWLY trace around the sides of the star with your finger, following the instructions as you go. **START HERE** and move in a clockwise direction.

This means pause for 2 or 3 seconds while holding your breath.

PAUSE

BREATHE OUT

BREATHE IN

BREATHE IN

BREATHE OUT

PAUSE

PAUSE

BREATHE OUT

BREATHE IN

BREATHE IN

BREATHE OUT

BREATHE OUT

BREATHE IN

PAUSE

PAUSE

BLOWING BUBBLES is another way of focusing on calm breathing.

If you run out of bubble mixture you could make your own.

To make the mixture, stir four tablespoons of dishwashing liquid into a cup of water.

CLEAN DISHES

Dip a bubble wand into the mixture, and slowly blow through the opening to create a stream of bubbles.

FLOAT

When you breathe deeply, you take in lots more oxygen. This helps to slow your heartbeat, stabilize your blood pressure and make you feel relaxed.

DRIFT

CLOUDSPOTTING

Sit and gaze at these clouds for a while.
Do any of them look like particular
shapes or pictures? Add words or draw
outlines depending on what you see.

Do you see animals? Countries? People?
Mythical creatures? Plants?

 ← WHALE

Now try cloudspotting outside too.
Sit outside, or look out of a window.
Get comfortable, relax, and look up for a while.

Use the space below to draw in any clouds you spot.

Add any thoughts buzzing around your head onto these blank clouds here...

WHOOOOSH

...then imagine them blowing away in the wind.

WHOOSH

WRITE IT OUT

Many people use lists as tools to declutter and CALM their minds. Try it out here.

I'M LOOKING FORWARD TO...

I LIKE TO EAT...

Scientists believe focusing on POSITIVE things releases chemicals in your brain that make it easier to RELAX.

I LOVE...

·····································
·····································
·····································
·····································
·····································
·····································
·····································
·····································
·····································
·····································
·····································
·····································
·····································
·····································
·····································
·····································
·····································

Here's a blank list. Write down more stuff you love, or anything you worry about, or things rushing around your head...

·····································
·····································
·····································
·····································
·····································
·····································
·····································
·····································
·····································
·····································
·····································
·····································
·····································
·····································
·····································
·····································
·····································
·····································
·····································
·····································
·····································

NAPS
Z Z Z Z

LEAVES

SUNSET

MORE
NAPS
Z Z Z Z

LOOK INSIDE

There's a centuries-old method of keeping calm, called MEDITATION. It wakes up parts of your brain that help you grow AWARE of your body, thoughts and emotions. This can help make busy, stressful thoughts feel much smaller.

There are hundreds of
different ways to meditate.
For a lot of them, you sit like this...

FACING FORWARD

EYES CLOSED

ARMS AND
SHOULDERS RELAXED

HANDS RESTING
ON KNEES

LEGS CROSSED

BACK STRAIGHT

Prop up your bottom, legs and knees with cushions, if it's uncomfortable.

Once you're comfortable, try this meditation technique. Focus on your body as you do it.

1

Breathe in through your nose, then open your mouth like this, and as you breathe out say...

AAAAAAAA...

2

Slowly close your mouth and the sound will start to change to...

...UHHHHH...

3

Keep closing your mouth until it's fully closed. The sound will change to...

...MMMM...

4

When you join these sounds together slowly, over and over again, you might feel different parts of your body

BUZZ and VIBRATE.

Your muscles might relax, too.

The more you try it, the easier it will get...

ROUND AND ROUND

START

Take a
moment to
follow this
path with your
pencil, as it
slowly winds its
way to the middle
of the picture.

FINISH

A maze with only one path is called a labyrinth. It's soothing because it requires concentration to follow the loops – but you CAN'T go wrong.

SLOW BAKING

Baking bread is a restful type of cooking, because you can't RUSH it. Dough needs time to rest and rise before you bake it. Follow this recipe to see for yourself.

INGREDIENTS
FOR 12 ROLLS:

450g (1lb) strong white bread flour

1 teaspoon of salt

2 teaspoons of fast-action yeast

300ml (1/2 pint) warm water, which has been boiled and cooled a bit

2 tablespoons olive or vegetable oil

EQUIPMENT:

Measuring cup or jug

Wooden spoon

Baking tray

Wire rack

Mixing bowl

Dish cloth

Kitchen towel

Oven and oven gloves

Check with your grown-up that it's okay for you to use the oven. They might even want to join in!

RECIPE:

1. MIX IT...

Mix the flour, salt and yeast in the mixing bowl.

Make a HOLE in the middle of the flour mix. Pour in the water and oil, and stir it all together to make soft, squidgy DOUGH.

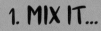

2. PRESS IT...

Dust a clean surface with flour and place the dough on top.

Push down into the middle of the dough to flatten and stretch it...

...then fold it in half...

...and push it down again.

This process is known as KNEADING.

Keep on kneading for around 10 minutes, until the dough feels smooth and springy.

3. LEAVE IT...

Put the dough in the mixing bowl, cover the top with a clean, damp dish cloth, and leave it for 1-2 hours.

Don't rush this part. The dough should DOUBLE in size.

4. TEAR IT...

Divide the dough into 12 pieces and roll each one into a ball.

Wipe a thin layer of butter onto the baking tray, using a clean piece of kitchen towel. Then, place the dough balls on the tray.

5. LEAVE IT AGAIN...

Leave the balls to rise in a warm place, uncovered, for around 40 minutes.

Meanwhile, heat the oven to 220°C (425°F, or gas mark 7).

VOILA! The rolls are ready.

6. BAKE THEM...

for 12-15 minutes.

Now leave them to cool on a wire rack.

GET LOST IN A TALE...

Use the pictures around the page as inspiration, and get writing. Take yourself away for a while as you write a whole story, a start, an ending, a song or even a poem. Just use words to tell a tale.

THE PAST

You could use some of these words to inspire you.

CASTLE   CITY   DREAM   ADVENTURE   ICE   SEA   PAST

FUTURE CROWN WOODS JOURNEY PATHWAY STORM ESCAPE CHAINS

MAGIC

VOYAGE

SLEEP

MOUNTAIN

METAL

POWER

CHAOS

FEAST

ENCHANTED

COMBAT   WINDOWS   LOST   HEROIC   RAMSHACKLE   DRIZZLE   LEGEND   FOREST

MANDALA

A MANDALA is a circular design made up of repeating shapes and patterns. For centuries, people all around the world have seen it as a symbol of calm and harmony.

Shade in this mandala, choosing colours that make you feel peaceful and relaxed.

The word 'mandala' means circle in Sanskrit, an ancient Indian language.

Have a go at completing this mandala by filling it with flowing shapes and lines.

Take it slooooowly – draw one shape at a time in each section of the mandala. And don't worry, it doesn't have to look perfect.

The key to it is REPETITION – the shapes in this section need to appear in the same place in every other section.

LAYER UPON LAYER

Find a paintbrush, water, some paints and a piece of paper.
Then paint a landscape, very gradually, one layer at a time.

Here's how to paint a range of mountains,
some in the foreground, some far, far away.

Pick a colour. Mix it with
white paint, or water it down,
to make it as pale as possible.

Paint the entire piece of
paper that colour, then
WAIT...

Once the first layer has DRIED,
mix a slightly darker version of it,
then paint the most distant
layer of mountains.

With each new layer,
paint all the way to the
bottom of the page, then
WAIT...

You could use the time
between layers to relax,
or to try some more
unhurry activities.

After the previous layer
has dried, add a slightly
DARKER layer on top...

...so that the colours get
darker and darker, the nearer
you are to the foreground...

...until you run out of space.

44

YOU COULD USE THE SAME TECHNIQUE TO CREATE...

...a city skyline.

...desert dunes.

...ocean waves.

CUT AND PASTE STORIES

Dig out an old magazine or newspaper, and look slowly through it for words and phrases you like. Cut them out, then take some time to turn them into a cut-and-paste story.

You could use the words to spark ideas...

rainforest

MYSTERY

She was deeper into the jungle than any human had ever been before. And she was frightened...

...make an entire story out of cut-up words...

Standing on the SPANISH castle WALL they COULD SEE ...

...or write your own words in between to make sentences.

The president rode along a DESERT path on his faithful WILDEBEEST .

Take your time going through a newspaper to find the most interesting or inspiring words you can...

SLOTH EXPRESS

47

MAKE A DEN

Nestle down with a book or notebook when you need some quiet time to yourself. Here are some ideas for making a COMFY space to rest and relax in.

Curl up in a soft sheet or duvet.

Drape a sheet over two chairs and crawl in.

Add decorations.

Cushions

You could make a
den outdoors.

Prop branches in
a ring around a
tree trunk.

The space you're in
can change the way
you feel and think.
It's usually easier to
relax when it's quiet
and you're feeling
comfortable.

Add dried
leaves to make
a soft floor.

Tie a washing line or string between two
trees and drape a sheet over it.

SHHH
QUIET ZONE

Place stones on the
corners to weigh
them down.

49

SHADE IN SHADES

Finish off these sunglasses by shading in the lenses. Start with a very light tint and then get darker and darker – until the last pair is almost black.

Psychologists have found that simple, repetitive actions such as shading can be COMFORTING. You don't have to think too much, let your hand do the work instead.

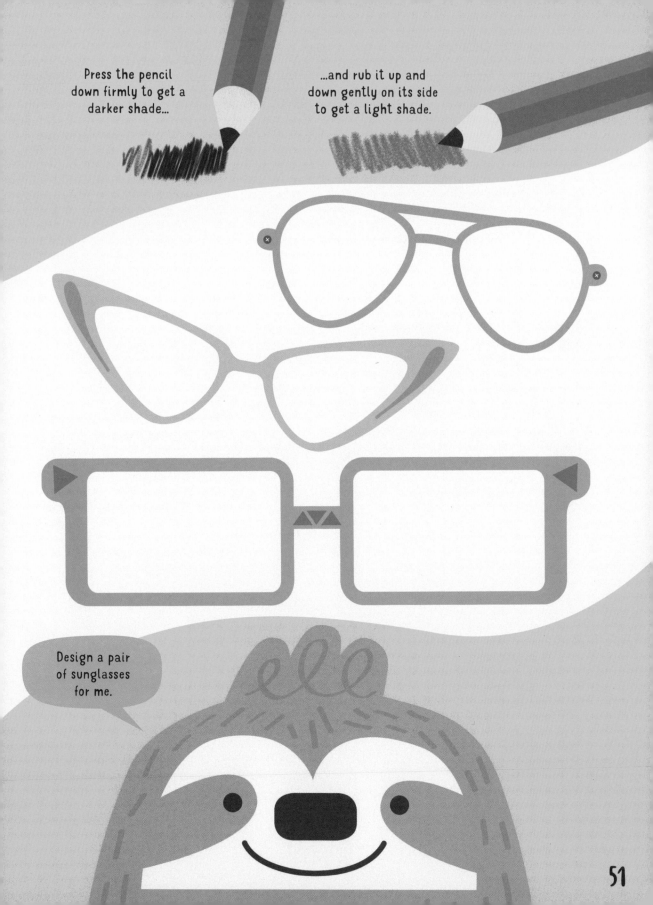

Press the pencil down firmly to get a darker shade...

...and rub it up and down gently on its side to get a light shade.

Design a pair of sunglasses for me.

51

FLAT ON YOUR BACK

When you're lying down FLAT, you're in the best position to relax. Give these flat-on-your-back relaxation techniques a try.

BELLY BALLOON

1

Lie on your back and place your hands on your tummy. Imagine your tummy is an empty balloon.

2

Breathe in through your NOSE and count to four. Feel your tummy fill up with air.

3

Count to two, then slowly breathe out through your MOUTH. Your tummy should deflate.

4

Wait a few seconds, then repeat a few times.

Breathing into your tummy makes you take slower, deeper breaths. This makes your heart beat slower, and your muscles relax. In fact, it might even send you to sleep.

TENSE, UNTENSE

1
Lie down with your arms on either side of you, with all of your muscles loose.

These activities release calming, feel-good chemicals into your brain and muscles. The chemicals overpower other chemicals, such as ADRENALINE, which keep you tense and alert.

2
Take a slow, deep breath in, then TENSE your WHOLE BODY (but not so much that it hurts) and count to four...

3
...then UNTENSE it all at once. Repeat this several times.

HUG YOURSELF

1
Lie down so that you're comfy, and give yourself a BIG HUG.

2
Close your eyes and focus on your breathing. After a short while, you'll probably notice yourself feeling calmer.

GROW A SEED

Grow a plant from a tiny seed. You only need a handful of compost, a dash of water, sunshine and... some TIME. Nature can't be hurried – seeds grow at their own pace.

1

First, you need a seed – any seed. Here are some seeds you might find in your kitchen.

PUMPKIN SEEDS

WHOLE LENTILS

CORN KERNELS

CUMIN SEEDS

APPLE, TOMATO OR LEMON SEEDS

Carefully cut open the fruit and extract the seeds. Leave them to dry out at room temperature before planting them.

2

Next, fill a container, such as an empty yogurt carton, with compost.

Leave a bit of room at the top of the carton.

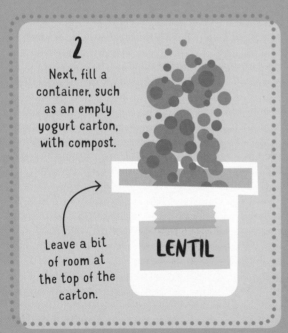

LENTIL

3

Push a couple of seeds in and spread them all out.

Sprinkle some compost on top to cover them.

LENTIL

54

A seed needs LIGHT
and WATER to grow.

4

Put the carton
by a window with
lots of light or in
a sheltered spot
outside.

LENTIL

5

CARE for your seed by giving
it a little water every day,
so the compost feels damp
to the touch.

Some seeds never grow, so don't
worry if you don't see anything.
Just try with another seed.

It will take several days, or even weeks, for small
shoots to appear. Keep track of your seed's progress
by sketching it at different points.

DATE:..............................

DATE:..............................

DATE:..............................

Using plants and gardens
to improve your physical
and mental health is called
GARDENING THERAPY. Growing
green things helps people slow
down and live in the moment –
and it's satisfying too.

FOLD A DOVE

There's a gentle magic to folding a piece of paper and seeing it gradually turn into something else.

Follow these instructions to have a go at the ancient Japanese art of paper folding, known as ORIGAMI, and make a paper dove.

You will need a square piece of paper. Here's how to make one from a rectangular piece of paper.

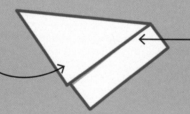

Fold one corner to the opposite edge.

Use a ruler to draw a line at the bottom edge of the triangle, then cut along it.

1

Fold the square in half, corner to corner.

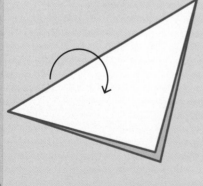

2

Then fold it in half again, corner to corner.

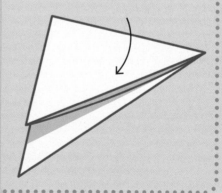

3

Top layer only, fold the point at the bottom up to meet the top-right corner.

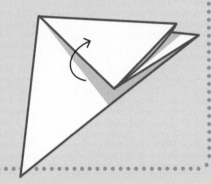

4

Turn the paper over and repeat step 3.

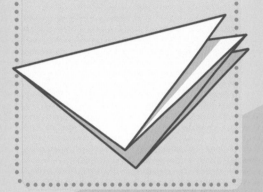

5

Top layer only, fold the lower corner up to meet the top edge. Then unfold it.

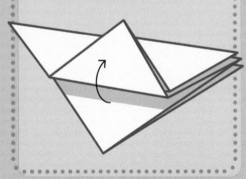

6

Lift the top-right point, then push the bottom corner in and flatten the model along the fold lines you made in step 5.

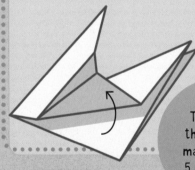

This turns the fold you made in step 5 inside out.

If you're finding any of the steps tricky, take a big, slow breath and try again.

This is how step 6 should end up looking.

7

Turn the paper over, and repeat steps 5 and 6 on the other side of the paper.

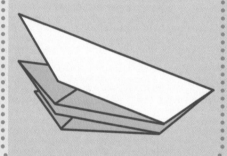

8

Fold down the closed point on the right like this, then unfold.

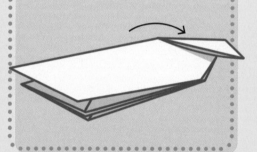

9

Slightly lift up the top layer, then push the right corner in between the two layers. Flatten along the creases you made in step 8.

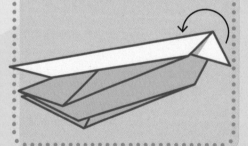

10

Swing the bottom-left point up, top layer only, to make the wing.

Repeat on the other side.

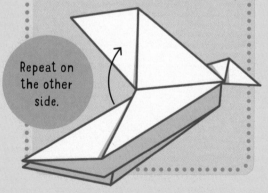

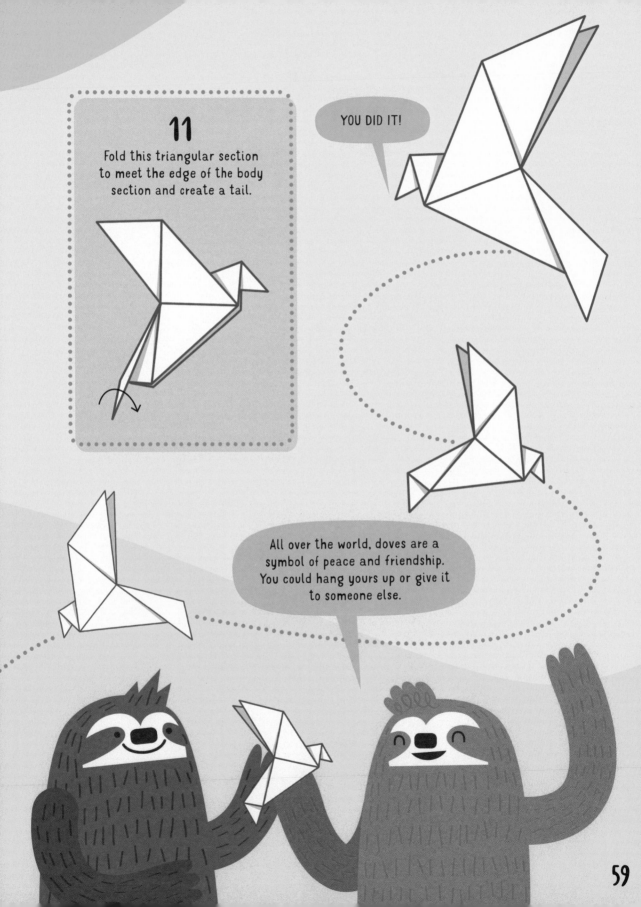

11

Fold this triangular section to meet the edge of the body section and create a tail.

YOU DID IT!

All over the world, doves are a symbol of peace and friendship. You could hang yours up or give it to someone else.

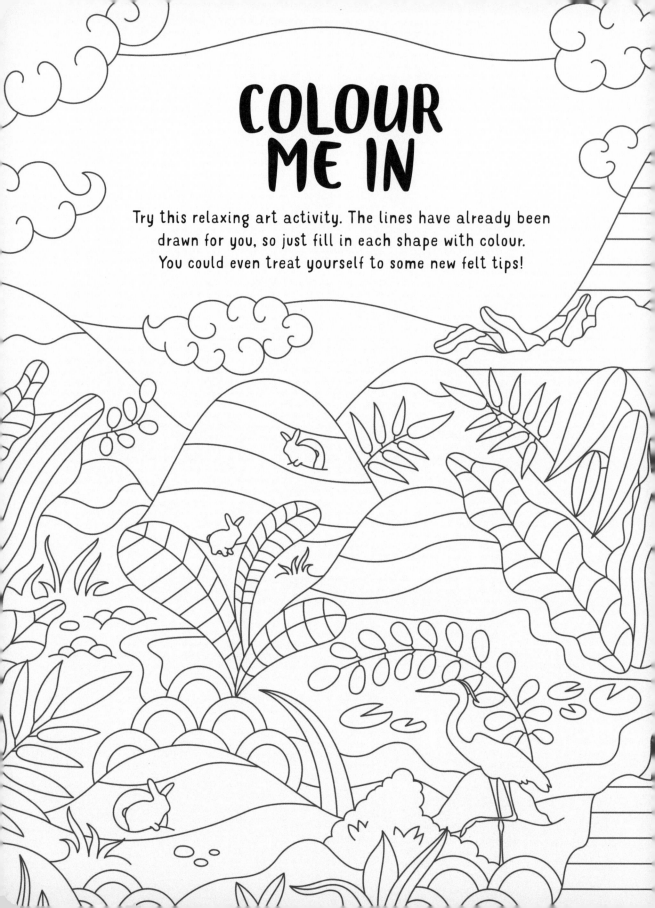

COLOUR ME IN

Try this relaxing art activity. The lines have already been
drawn for you, so just fill in each shape with colour.
You could even treat yourself to some new felt tips!

ARE WE THERE YET?

Sometimes on a long journey you just want to GET THERE. But you can't do anything to rush or hurry the journey... Here are some games to play on the way.

I DON'T SPY

Try playing 'I Spy', but don't limit it to what you can see. Think of ANYTHING, and get other people to ask for clues until they guess what it is.

Can you eat it?

Is it an animal?

It might take a little while...

Where is it?

BEEP

Can it talk?

STORY CHAIN

Take it in turns to tell a story, one sentence at a time. The story can go on and on for as long as you like...

Once upon a time, there was a sloth, who lived in the tallest tree in the land.

Every day the sloth climbed up and up, but it never reached the top...

Little did the sloth know, that at the top lived... a KING.

A BUMPY PORTRAIT

Cars and trains can be bouncy places. Have a go at a lumpy, bumpy SELF PORTRAIT as you travel on your journey. Don't worry about getting it perfect - embrace the rocky ride.

IN BALANCE

Solving a puzzle takes focus and patience. Use a pencil and eraser to solve these maths puzzles at your own pace.

Write in a number on the blank shapes, so that each mobile balances. Both sides of the mobile need to add up to the same amount.

On each mobile, shapes that look the same have the same number.

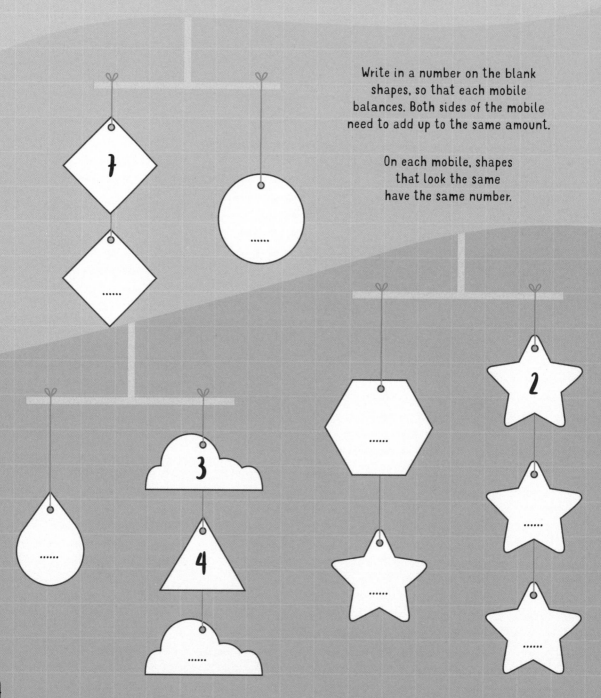

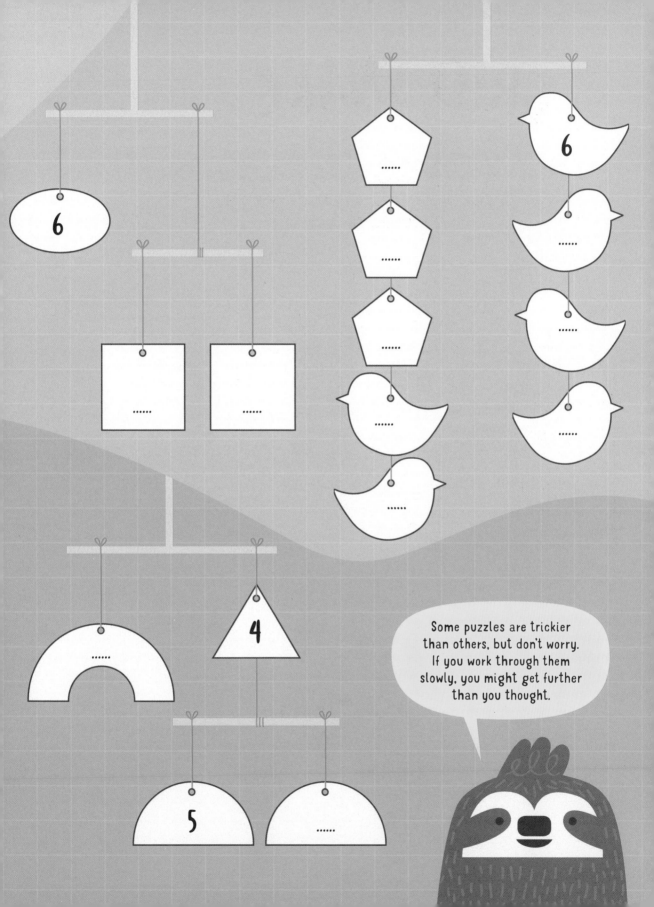

Some puzzles are trickier than others, but don't worry. If you work through them slowly, you might get further than you thought.

GRID SNAKE

Keep this line going, and make it snake right
across the page, always sticking to the grid.
Try to pass through ALL the dots as your line
creeps around the page.

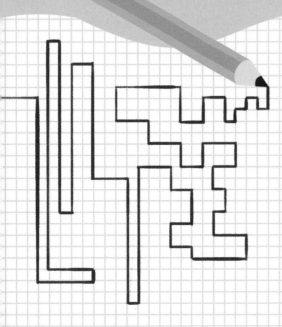

This grid is very small, so you'll have to draw carefully and take your time. There's no right way to do it - just try to hit all the dots.

MASSAGE PACK

MASSAGES can relax your muscles, calm your nerves, and even help you sleep better. Get comfy and try these massage techniques on yourself.

HEAD

Place the tips of your fingers on your head, like this.

Rub your fingers around all at once, as if you're rubbing in shampoo.

Keep going for as long as you feel like.

ARMS

Pressing gently with one hand, make long, flowing strokes up and down your arm, from your wrist to your shoulder. Do this until you feel your arm warm up.

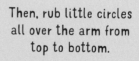

Then, rub little circles all over the arm from top to bottom.

Try these techniques on both arms, and then on both legs too.

FEET

Find a soft ball, such as a tennis ball, and place one foot on it.

Roll the ball forwards and backwards with your foot for a while...

...then try rolling it around in little circles, all along your foot.

Try it on both feet - but not at once!

SHOULDERS

Relax your shoulders, then rub up and down one of them until the shoulder feels warm.

Next, move up and down the same shoulder, making light, short squeezes as you go.

Do this on both shoulders, one at a time.

Stressful feelings aren't just in your mind - they make your BODY tense, too. Massaging tense parts of your body can make stressful feelings shrink.

FIND UNHURRY

Search for the words on the right-hand side in this big jumble of letters. Look across, up, down or backwards to find them.

```
B N E W R H L A X R
R E U E I K D V R O
E N V C V S N B V A
C L N D U L A S X T
S U G W I O U P R M
L R U Z A W H V T E
O A D G H O X E R D
R E C H A R G E E I
M T E A U N V F E T
O E Z O O N S H G A
J N V I N T H U L T
B R E U T I M E A E
R N U N H U R R Y W
E V U W S H A V E N
C A R I T R V H A U
Z U R N O S P A T L
A I M D N E F K E Z
```

UNHURRY RELAX RECHARGE UNWIND
REGROUP BREATHE SLOW CALM SLOTH
STRETCH SNOOZE CHILL MEDITATE

```
T  F  A  R  V  E  C  A  C  O
A  G  R  D  A  O  H  A  H  F
P  C  L  N  L  D  A  R  I  G
U  S  O  L  W  Y  R  N  L  E
O  W  I  N  D  S  U  R  L  R
R  E  A  T  M  L  A  C  U  Y
G  R  E  L  A  N  J  A  G  N
E  Y  F  U  N  P  S  O  B  H
R  E  L  A  X  C  T  M  R  L
S  M  U  D  A  R  R  H  E  R
U  R  N  L  A  X  E  A  A  Y
C  K  I  E  R  E  T  R  T  R
R  T  Y  U  D  V  C  G  H  U
N  V  O  A  T  H  H  V  E  N
S  H  N  A  O  R  V  E  L  L
H  A  B  R  E  T  Y  H  R  U
G  E  N  T  L  S  L  O  T  H
```

BEACH CHILL

Wherever you are, imagine waves lap the shore, a breeze wafts across the warm sand and you are slowly eating a delicious ice cream. Add colour and detail to this lazy day at the beach.

Add some colour to the waves.

What is she dreaming about?

Decorate the castle with shells.

What are the flavours?

73

MOON DIARY

Looking at the night sky before bed can help you unwind. That's because your body is programmed to slow down and feel sleepy when it's dark.

Look up at the Moon and draw its shape in the first box below. Draw it again the next night, and the nights after that, to keep track of how it changes.

Can you see any craters or bumps?

On a cloudy night, if you can't see the Moon, just draw in clouds. You might be able to spot a glow where the Moon is hiding.

The Moon doesn't actually change shape, it just looks as if it does. That's because it moves around the Earth and is lit up by the Sun from different angles.

It will take about 28 nights for the Moon to look as it did in your first box. This means it has completed a full circle around the Earth. It's a cycle that is repeated night after night – so you can always look up and check in on what the Moon's up to.

SLEEPY HEAD

Sometimes it's hard to slow your brain before bed. Sticking to a BEDTIME ROUTINE can help to bring on sleepiness.

You could...

...TURN OFF SCREENS

Try not to look at a TV, phone or computer before going to sleep, and don't keep any screens by your bed.

The light of a screen makes it harder for your brain to produce MELATONIN - the chemical that makes you feel sleepy.

...HAVE A WARM BATH OR SHOWER

The warm water relaxes your muscles. Afterwards, as you cool down, your body reaches a good temperature for sleep.

...WRITE IT 'OUT'

If your head is full of whirring thoughts, try writing them down. Then you can let go of them until the morning.

...DIM THE LIGHTS

Switch off bright lights. Low light sends a signal to your brain that it's time to wind down.

If you find it really hard to sleep most nights, speak to a grown-up. They may be able to give you more tips and help.

There isn't a perfect recipe for falling asleep. Often, focusing on something can help you to relax and drift off. See if one of these techniques works for you.

For some people counting sheep really does work.

Start a story in your head and add to it every night.

Imagine your body is a city and the lights are all on. Then imagine the lights slowly switching off at your toes, and then at your ankles, knees, hips, tummy, chest – up to the top of your head.

You might even fall asleep before all the lights are turned off.

Fill an imaginary room with relaxing furniture and comforting things.

Try not to get frustrated if it takes a while to fall asleep. It makes it harder to unwind. Relaxing in bed is still good rest, even if you're not quite asleep yet.

SLOW AS A SLOTH

Sloths are tree-dwelling mammals noted for their SLOWNESS. Their days are spent eating (slowly) and resting (a lot). Learn about these leisurely animals in this quiz.

1 The fastest humans can complete a 100m race in under 10 seconds. It would take a sloth...

- [ ] ...10 minutes.
- [ ] ...20 minutes.
- [ ] ...33 minutes.

2 One reason sloths are so slow is because...

- [ ] ...they don't get much energy from the leaves they eat.
- [ ] ...they don't want to frighten each other by moving too quickly.
- [ ] ...they need to save their energy for dancing at the full moon.

Zzzzzzzzz

3 Sloths sleep for...

- [ ] ...5 hours a day.
- [ ] ...10 hours a day.
- [ ] ...around 15 hours a day.

4 How long does it take a sloth to digest a big, leafy meal?

- ☐ 6 hours
- ☐ 12 hours
- ☐ A week or more

> You busy humans should really take a leaf out of our book.

5 Sloths move so little that moss-like algae grows on their fur. This is useful...

- ☐ ...as a tasty snack for when the sloth gets hungry.
- ☐ ...as camouflage in its rainforest home.
- ☐ ...to attract a mate.

6 How often do sloths climb down to the ground?

- ☐ Every week to go to the toilet
- ☐ Once a year to have a bubble bath
- ☐ Never

7 Sloths' strong claws help them to...

- ☐ ...comb their fur.
- ☐ ...tickle their young.
- ☐ ...spend most of their time hanging upside down.

> You'll find the answers on the next page.

ANSWERS

Pages 64-65 IN BALANCE
The hanging mobiles balance like this.

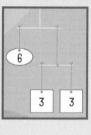

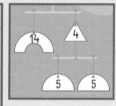

Pages 70-71 FIND UNHURRY

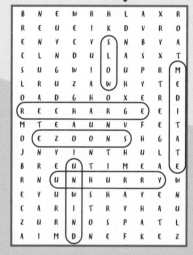
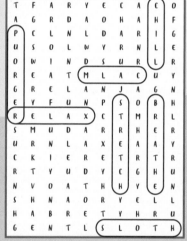

Pages 78-79 SLOW AS A SLOTH
1. 33 minutes 2. They don't get much energy from the leaves 3. Around 15 hours
4. A week or more 5. Camouflage 6. Every week 7. Their claws help them to hang upside down.

Designed by:
Tom Ashton-Booth, Freya Harrison, Claire Morgan, Jenny Offley and Eleanor Stevenson
With additional illustration by Tom Ashton-Booth
Series editor: Jane Chisholm
Series designer: Stephen Moncrieff